I0698493

MORTGAGE ENTREPRENEUR 101

You Don't Have A Job,
You Run A Million Dollar Business.

By AJ Nunnally

Table of Contents

Foreward

I have known and worked with AJ Nunnally for over 15 years. I consider him a dear friend and one of my best mortgage industry resources. AJ not only stays up to date on various loan programs, he is also extremely passionate about assisting individuals in achieving home ownership. He also has been known to recruit, train and lead successful mortgage teams.

Stephanie Prentice, REALTOR®, SRES®
Managing Broker
Licensed in the Commonwealth of Virginia
United Real Estate Richmond

Acknowledgement

This book is dedicated to my parents Albert J. Nunnally Jr. and Betty M. Nunnally. To my father (My Dude man), as I affectionately called him, you taught me how to be a man. You were my first best friend. You taught me how to always be honest and frank with people. Family, friends, and even our local pastor knew exactly what was on your mind; you held nothing back.

You always provided a roof over my head and food to eat. I was born and grew up in the same house that my mother still resides in today, almost 54 years later, you built that house. When I was about 5 years old, you decided we needed more room, so you took the roofing system off and added another level. It was then that my love for construction was born.

Thank you for telling me, "No," when I need it. Thank you for always being there for me at every first in my life. You were there when I fell on the glass dish while feeding the dog (requiring about 30 stitches), you helped me purchase my first moped and my first car, you taught me how to catch my first fish. You were there when I drove my first boat. You paid my way through college, you were there when I bought my first house and my first investment property, you helped me to build my first property and open two businesses. You were my father, mentor, and best friend all in one.

To my mother who took me everywhere she went for the first five years of my life: you taught me the importance of family. You are my biggest fan. Sometimes when my dad said, "No", you would still make things happen. You came to all my football, baseball, and tennis games even though you knew nothing about sports. You took me and my friends to the movies, pizza night, skating, and even Bingo every weekend. When I got my first car you helped me purchase it and fix it up.

In college when I could not work at the car wash because of the rain, you told me to come home so that you could care for me. You sold dinners and gave me the money to go back to school. When my first daughter was born, you knew that I was clueless about raising a child, you came to my house and sat with me until my ex-wife came back home. Meghan and I thank you.

When I over-extended myself financially and had to forfeit my car, you helped me get it back. You continued to believe in me and support me when I had to sell and lose almost everything I owned in my divorce. You encouraged me to get up and start over again. You taught me to put my faith in God and not man. Strong Faith, Strong Finish!

Thank you for praying over my life for fifty-four years. I know that you prayed over me before I was conceived. You will continue to pray for me until God calls one of us home. I love you from the bottom of my heart.

To my wife who taught me how to live life more purposely. You taught me that money and material things don't define me. We had some of the best times with about ten dollars between us both. Look at us now! God is good! You always remind me that you loved me first and I was the one trying not to fall in love with you. We both see how that ended. Living my life with you makes me push harder and enjoy our time together even more. You are definitely my dad in a girl version. I can see the similarities between you and my dad quite clearly. You never hesitate to tell me the truth and establish boundaries; you hold nothing back.

To all my grandparents, aunts and uncles, the Blandford Community, and City of Petersburg who watched over my life: Thank you. A special thanks for my favorite great aunt, Alice Campbell aka Aunt Neale. I would like to extend special thanks to my grandmother, Christine Nunnally aka Gauni, my grandfather Albert Nunnally, Sr. aka Gumbo Shorty, my other grandmother Lucille McKeever, and grandfather George McKeever. To my all my aunts, RIH Laverne Smith aka Aunt Mammie &
RIH to Aunt Helen Bennett, and all my uncles RIH-Deacon Lawrence McKeever aka Uncle Pa, my first spiritual mentor. RIH George McKeever aka King George.

To my children Meghan, Terrance, Essence and Tyne', thank you all for being patient with me as I learn how to love you all unconditionally. I am proud of you all. Keep seeking out your purpose in life while letting God guide your steps. To my two grandsons, I thank you for bringing some more testosterone into the house. I can't wait until we can go fishing together on my new boat. I'm claiming that God will provide the Nunnally family a new boat. Amen!

To my Best friends Al Beamon, Jeff Sumpter, Emanuel Batts, and

Derek Morris, I love you guys from the bottom of my heart. To my Dear Fraternity Omega Psi Phi, Fraternity, Inc and my line brothers Bernard Fitzgerald and Sherman Wilkins, we have a bond for life. Spring 89 of Tau Lambda Chapter of Old Dominion University: Thank you, God, my family, and Omega for molding me into the man that I am becoming. My First Mortgage Mentor. Mrs. Nancy Burkett, thank you for teaching me the mortgage business while working at another company. Who would know that what started as a job would become a 31-year business/career?

To the Blandford Community and the City of Petersburg: thank you for showing me that I could do something with my life. I learned at a early age that it is not where you are but where you are going.

Last, but not least, my cousin Rodney Jones, I love you unconditionally. Thank you for encouraging me be so much more in life.

I will be a better man, spiritually, a better husband to my wife, a better father and grandfather, a better son, a better friend, and a better mentor. I can be a better person to everyone I meet. I'm becoming a servant leader.

You have given me my freedom. I will no longer compete against the world. I will seek God's wisdom in everything I do, help and mentor everything that God places in my life, and work on building a legacy for 200 years.

I want to build legacy for 4 generations of my family. I will study the word to show my self-approved. I will study my business and master my purpose. I will seek wisdom from life coaches, business coaches, and spiritual coaches and friends. Let's Go!

Chapter One:
Did God Create Me to Be
A Mortgage Loan Officer?

I grew up in Petersburg, Virginia, a small city with a population of 30,000. I was always good at math and I read only when I was required to read . Until recently, I would only read books for class or to take tests. My love has always been numbers, counting, and math calculations. I realized that I was good at math when I entered high school and basic math lead me to algebra, trigonometry, calculus, and geometry. I did not want to master math, I simply enjoyed working with numbers.

I majored in accounting. Although I was great at math, I realized that I was not going to become an accountant after several attempts to master the coursework. I received an AC in my third accounting course to continue my major in accounting. I spent a year lowering my GPA to academic probation before I threw in the towel on my accounting dream.

I began to study finance and this included classes in banking, stock brokerage, real estate, and insurance. I always enjoyed my real estate financing classes the most. Fast forward to graduating from Old Dominion in December 1991, it took me 4 1/2 years to complete this journey. I was on academic preparation twice, I failed a few classes, was suspended for one year, and attended VCU to continue my education.

In the spring of 1989, I joined the greatest fraternity in the world, Omega Psi Phi Fraternity Incorporated at Old Dominion University. I would like to acknowledge the Ques and the sisters of Delta Sigma Theta. Sending much love to the Divine 9. We all do great things for this world.

While unloading trucks at Walmart Distribution Center I desired to build a career at Walmart. I wanted to move up from trainer, supervisor, management, and distribution center general manager. I also obtained my real estate license in 1992 while working at Walmart Distribution Center. The politics of corporate America and racism let me know then that this was not for me. In 1993 one of my ex-wife friends was working at Crestar Bank in the mortgage department. She asked me if I wanted to get a job as a loan officer. I did not know what the job entailed. However, I did know that whatever the job description, it had to be better than unloading trucks at Walmart Distribution Center. I went to the interview, landed the job and was well on my way to a career in mortgages, so I thought. I spent the next three to six months answering phone calls. Crestar was so busy trying to help keep customers in their homes that no one had time to train me. My duties at Crestar included answering the phones and getting mail. I would sort through the mail daily. We were bombarded with house keys accompanied by letters relinquishing houses back to the mortgage company due to the inability to pay. Most of these clients had high interest rates or adjustable-rate mortgages and were not able to continue to make their mortgage payments. The main problem was that they were upside down in equity in their homes. This means that they owed more money than homes were worth. Banks were not allowing them to refinance to the existing lower interest rates. With so many families facing the same fate, the government introduced new rules which allowed us to refinance homes without an appraisal. This helped millions of families save their homes.

I could only think about the families that had been mailing me keys for the last year. I realized that there was a disproportionate amount of minorities and low to middle income homeowners that lost their homes and had their families displaced. I vowed to help anyone who wanted to become a homeowner or anyone who was trying to keep their home. That is when my journey as a loan officer began.

This is when the Federal Government allowed the Banks and Mortgage Companies to refinance homes without appraisal value restrictions. This was my first refinance boom. The floodgates opened with new clientele, we were busy for about a year. I could not stop thinking about the keys the letters and the families that did not make it until the rules of the mortgage game could change to help them. Most of these families were low and moderate income to middle income families. The really poor people did not own homes and the rich could keep making payments or could pay their homes off completely. The middle class was left suffering.

While sitting at my desk one day a stranger called. He introduced himself as Howard Dalton, manager of First Colonial

Bank in Prince George, Virginia. They were looking to recruit loan officers. I really loved my job at Crestar and did not want to leave. One day during my lunch hour, my supervisor commented that he saw great potential in me. He said that I had potential to be a street loan officer. I told him about the recruiting call I had received. He let me know that I would probably be jobless once interest rates raised and all of our clients were refinanced. He was retired and only did this for extra income, so he was looking forward to the job ending. He wanted to get back to his retired life. He suggested that I go on the interview and look at becoming what he called a street loan officer. A street loan officer works outside of the bank and and meets with referral partners like realtors, builders and insurance agents to refer business to them and to get business from them.

I traveled down to Prince George, VA, interviewed with Hal Dalton and landed the job as a street loan officer. The year was 1993. I had a small salary and a small commission. I would meet with realtors, builders, and do community service in the area each day. I knew very little about mortgage programs, guidelines, and how to do business as a loan officer. I was about 23 years old and my salary was 30K to $40K per year plus a small commission. Growing up in Petersburg, VA, and being the first person in my immediate family to finish college, I thought I had made it. I was rich! This was the first time that I'd measured my success based on the lack of the success of others around me. I was the crab at the top of the bucket. I have since learned that comparison is never a good thing to do. You can only run your race, the race that God has created for you to run. If you run in someone else's lane you can never be successful and you'll be disqualified from the race.

After several months of trying to help families finance homes and trying to establish relationships with real estate agents that I knew, I began to realize how difficult the job was going to be. I thought that the agents in the office would give me their clients because I had my real estate license at century 21 CF Scott. I asked the agents at the office why they didn't send me their mortgage referrals and they chuckled. They told me that they didn't send referrals to me because I had no clue what I was doing. The reality was that they were absolutely correct. I was not a skilled at mortgages. I had a college degree in finance but had real experience with mortgage financing. I realized, right then, that I would need to study the guidelines for mortgage financing to master my career or I would struggle and have to find another job. If I wanted success at this business, I had to take the initiative myself. I decided to take control of the situation. I asked my boss to give me copies of the underwriting manuals. I wanted to shadow the underwriters and the processors. I studied the techniques of the loan officers that worked at other companies.

When I visited the Century 21 CF Scott office in Petersburg, one person was always a constant in the office. A loan officer named Nancy Burkett she was doing most of the mortgage business in the office. This was the same office that I thought was going to be in my domain for getting mortgage clients. I realized very quickly that Nancy was a master at mortgage lending. She dominated in that arena. She knew how to work the guidelines to help families become homeowners. Nancy was the one person who could get almost any difficult loan situation funded. I saw Nancy as a threat to my success. I was very intimidated by simply being in her presence. After months of struggling with this, I finally built up the courage to introduce myself to Nancy. Nancy was the branch manager at another mortgage company where she was very successful. She was one of their top loan officers in the area. Her response changed my life and my career in mortgage lending. The lady who I had been intimidated by for months, immediately offered to assist me to learning the mortgage business. She gave me her business card and told me to call her if I had any questions or needed help getting my clients financed. I could not believe her response. I believed that she was just pacifying me and that if I called her, she would never answer. After a month went by and I was still struggling with funding clients; I found Nancy's business card. I picked up the phone and called her at her office. I told Nancy about my struggles and that I needed help qualifying clients, completing my good faith estimates and completing my truth in lending disclosures. At this time all of these things were done by hand. We didn't have the assistance of the technology we have today. I got in my car and drove to Nancy's office for her help. This was just one of many times. I sat down at her desk while she looked at the files that I brought with me. She helped me structure them. She helped me write credit letters. She told me what program that worked best for the clients, and I began to close loans. Nancy Burkett is the reason that 30 years later when I meet new loan officers that work at other companies, I offer my assistance to them. I wan to help them be successful just as she helped me. I want to pay the kindness that was extended to me forward to other new agents. Thank you Nancy Burkett for helping me and my family establish a career that has spanned over 30 years and has made me millions of dollars.

When I first got into the mortgage business with a degree in finance, I realized (in karate terms) that I was a 'no belt'. After receiving my first job at First Colonial Bank, I did know some of the terminology but did not have a clear understanding of the business. I was promoted to a 'white belt' (rookie). Nancy Burkett was a 'black belt' or a master in the mortgage industry. I realized that I needed to surround myself with masters, 'black belts', and 'brown belts' in the mortgage industry. Nancy was my first coach, mentor, and advisor as I started my journey into mortgage lending. I had so many questions, but no one to give me answers. Most of the top realtors did not look like me and would not speak to me. They did not send me business referrals either. At that time in the mortgage and real estate industry, it was difficult to find black loan officers and realtors. The wonderful thing about Nancy Burkett was that despite being a part of the majority white industry, she was helpful to people of all ethnic backgrounds. She was very instrumental in assisting the underserved markets of Petersburg and the surrounding areas. All of the realtors loved her and she could get any loan closed. She loved helping minorities. None of that made sense to me because she didn't look like me. My neighborhood was 99% African American. The American African American realtors I did know from my brief real estate career in Petersburg all sent their business referrals to Nancy. I initially saw her as my competition, but soon learned that she was one of my greatest mentors. Nancy told me to read the underwriting manuals and keys that accompany them; keep a copy with you at all times. I still have the books and the underwriting manuals and the first HP 10B calculator that I've used to make a lot of money over the last 30 years.

I started joining associations and attending all realty and mortgage related functions. I love good parties with good food and alcohol, so that kind of networking was easy for me. I had no problem drinking with the best of them. I learned that well from my days at Old Dominion University.

I started to meet realtors that were willing to send me business. Though I was grateful for the new influx of clientele, I found that a majority of the people that were referred to me were difficult to find financing, because many of them had credit challenges. Nancy showed to what to look for and how do address the client's needs. Anything from what creditors were looking for, what bills the clients needed to pay off, the information I needed to include in credit letters and what would get my clients approved or denied for mortgages.

Chapter Two:
What Is My Why And Purpose?

Remember, most businesses fail in the first three to five years. Building a company or as I call it, a business within a business is hard work. Look at your employer as your parent company; you are like a subsidiary. Never sell the company unless your name is on the door. You are literally an intrapreneur. Intrapreneurship is simply entrepreneurship in an existing organization. In many ways, intrapreneurship is easier for an individual than entrepreneurship because it has the support of an existing organization. Is your name Rocket Mortgage, Truist or Bank of America? Of course not! So why are you promoting someone else's business?

I asked my daughter, my wife, and close friends what I should call myself for the score. I owned and ran a successful mortgage brokerage for about 10 years. With the mortgage meltdown I had to close both my mortgage and my construction companies. Both of those businesses allowed me to see myself as an entrepreneur and I never will see myself as an employee again. Golden Heart Mortgage was the name of the mortgage company and Golden Heart Construction was the name of the construction company that I owned. I got the name from one of my favorite people on earth, my Aunt Neale. She was a mother, a grandmother, and my best friend. My Aunt Neale was a widow who took care of her sisters and brothers in Bronx, NY. She had no biological children, but she adopted me from the day I was born.

I remember my aunt owning several cars even though she didn't have a driver's license. She always allowed a family member with a license to use her cars for transportation and to take her where she needed to go. She was very resourceful. I remember us going to visit friends and family in the hospital. Aunt Neale took food to families on our journeys from Virginia to New York and back.

She was always making sure that I was well taken care of. She made sure that I had food and a place to stay in New York. The last time I visited her in the hospital, she showed me how to build generations of wealth before I even knew what it meant.

She passed away and left me my first house as an investment property. My legacy began at her memorial service in New York City. There were about 100 people in a Chapel. During her memorial service, everyone carried signs calling her the lady with a golden heart.

Ten different people spoke about the great things that Aunt Neale had done over the years. She had taken homeless men to cash their checks when they didn't have identification. She always promoted and pushed for equality and rights in the housing projects where she lived. There were close to 20,000 people living in that community.

It was then that I told my father, Albert Nunnally Jr. that If I ever got an opportunity to open a business I would name it Golden Heart after my Aunt Neale.

I decided that I wanted to own my own mortgage loan company. God blessed me with the opportunity to open Golden Heart Mortgage and Golden Heart Construction in honor of my late great Aunt Neale (Alice Campbell, rest in peace Aunt Neale). *Love you to death and thank you for molding me into the man I have become.* She was a great example of a servant leader.

Ok it is time to discuss how I became a successful Mortgage Entrepreneur and if this is the right career for you. The next step for me was finding an online or in person mortgage class and studying the details of the mortgage business.

If you choose to go this route you will need to take 20 hours of coursework, pass the exam, take a state and federal exam, and get sponsored by a mortgage company. You also have to pass a credit check and a background check before you will be officially licensed.

The MLS will issue you an MLS number. Some mortgage companies could require more classes and training requirements for other states. Each state is different. If you go to work for a bank or a credit union, they can sponsor you with no test required.

You might be thinking that if you go to work for a bank everything will be perfect. The answer to that is both yes and no. Remember, most banks only offer mortgage financing as one of many services. Some banks are very conservative when approving loans. Customer service could be compromised because you don't have many options.

You have more options when joining a mortgage brokerage. Mortgage brokers don't lend money, they offer products from banks, private lenders, commercial lenders, and others. They normally don't specialize in any one thing. They offer a myriad of mortgage financing options for a variety of client situations. They are really heavy on other companies to get mortgage deals approved. Some brokers are great at getting deals done. Some brokers are understaffed and have no offers. They are one-person marching bands. Another option is banks and credit unions. Some offer great mortgage products to the general public. Some only offer mortgages to their members or bank clients. Banks tend to be conservative in their underwriting guidelines and don't make decisions quickly. Sometimes they have great rates on certain programs but quick closings are not available.

Many times, they will also change direction, midstream, if news or market conditions are not favorable. As an employee of any institution, you are a number in the eyes of your employer. What matters to them is that you work 9:00 to 5:00 Monday through Friday and get an hour for lunch. If you don't like being micromanaged, become an entrepreneur. Another option is becoming a mortgage lender correspondent. A mortgage lender can be privately owned, owned by a corporation, or owned by a bank. These kinds of firms normally specialize in mortgage lending. Some even service their own loans meaning that you make your monthly payments to them. These companies offer their own mix of products, agency products like Fannie Mae, Freddie Mac FHA and VA, and specialized programs such as bank statement programs and construction perm financing.

New products that are being introduced to the market are DSC are loans and I10 loan specialty programs. These are my favorite choice of business. I can set up a company within a company. AJ3 Your Mortgage QB Team can exist within a larger company and take advantage of having access to the resources of the parent company and promoting their business.

In my case I look at myself as AJ3 Your Mortgage QB Team powered by New American (NAF). NAF is a large mortgage lender who services about 97% of their loans. They are about 93% minority in terms of employees and serve the disadvantaged communities.

When I found the opportunity, it was like I died and went to heaven. I found a company with almost 5000 employees that gave me a seat at the table on the train to home ownership in our underserved communities. Don't get me wrong. Everything isn't perfect, we have some growing to do. I have a foundation and a platform to build on.

This journey for me started 30 years ago. I thank the Lord for my purpose in life. If mortgages are not right for you and you want to consider a career in real estate, construction, insurance, or financial planning, we can guide you in that direction as well. We know the right folks to talk to.

Once you are ready to start this journey give me a call. I can help you become the king of your things. You can be one of the next Todd Duncans, Tim Braheems, Carl Whites, Rick Rubys, or the Bill Sparkmans of the world. All of these guys are Masters of Teaching about the mortgage industry, and some have similar styles. The one thing that all have that in common is as follows:

They have mastered the essential knowledge of the mortgage business. You must do the same. Know your programs and guidelines like an underwriter. Become an expert in what you're selling. Manage your time well. Be consistent with your daily tasks. Systems are the key to your success. Use the proper scripts. Find a mentor or coach.

Master techniques for ample lead generation. Some believe in cold calling no appointment visits, buying leads running ads, buying lists of qualified agents, radio ads, television ads, and others ways of finding leads. Do what you enjoy doing and what works for you and your company.

I prefer relationship building and networking. I enjoy being very strategic in selecting my business partners and working with people that I like and trust who also like and trust me.

I want my clients and referral partners to be customers for life and friends for life. Once you have mastered your why, begin to master the product guidelines and programs.

Start with the basics: conventional, FHA, VA and USDA loans. Master them all. You want to be like an underwriter in terms of program knowledge. If you have access to the top producer in your office or in your area, shadow them or let them become your mentor. Join their team. You may make less money, but it will be worth it in the end. Trust me, the top producer in your office should be your coach, your mentor, or your sensei.

The loan officer assistant, your loan processor, your loan processing assistant, your underwriter, and closer on your team if you can master the MLO and be good and have knowledge of processing, underwriting, and closing realtors and other mortgage loan officers.

A great assistant and processor are at the center of every great mortgage lending team. Similar to the medical field, nurses do 90% to 95% of the work. The doctor does his 5%, but his name is on the door. He leads the team. The doctor gets most of the credit.

A smart doctor takes great care of his team. His head nurse is appreciated or she will leave for a better environment or opportunity. She will choose to become a nurse practitioner or go back to medical school to start her own practice.

Take care of your team members and they will take care of you. Surprise them and spoil them with bonuses, trips, and training retreats. These are the things you should do for your team as a business owner.

Chapter Three:
Knowledge is Power

I have a degree in business with a concentration in finance. I also studied business accounting and marketing. I consider myself a pretty smart man. I have owned a few businesses. I'm doing just fine in life. I'm not bragging, I just know that I am truly blessed. I ran a mortgage company. I also currently help run a construction company. You must have strong faith and also strong action. (procrastination does not equal success).

I've never really had bulletproof system in place. I would come up with an idea, and go into it full force. I started a fire, then figured out how to extinguish it and get back on track. My parents, friends, and my business partners bailed me out of a difficult situation on more than one occasion. I thank God for His grace, mercy, and loyal family and friends.

I used to keep telling myself to work harder. However, the closer I looked at at the wealthiest people in the world, I realized that they worked the least. I realize that my wealth was not in my hands, but in my mind. Knowledge is money. Knowledge is POWER!

I started learning and reading every day. I listened audio books, read hardcover books, watched YouTube videos and listened to coaches and pastors. I pondered the million dollar question: How many of my teachers or professors had successfully run a business? I'm pretty sure the answer was none.

How can someone who was not a successful entrepreneur teach me how to become a successful entrepreneur? I had to unlearn some things that I was taught and change my way of thinking in order to run a successful mortgage business.

I desire financial freedom, deeper relationship with God, stronger faith, a recession proof business, and legacy building for my family. I have work to do in order to establish generational wealth for four generations.

Chapter Four:
Branding, Image & Integrity Matter

I hope that you have come up with a great name for your business. If your name is not on the building or the office door, then you should always brand yourself.

As you start to look into the future of how you want your business to be perceived by the public, I want you to memorize two important words. The first word is **shortcut**.

The definition of short cut is as follows: "A route more direct than the one ordinarily taken". I want to make sure that we are perfectly clear. I'm not saying that if you have a more efficient way of getting things done that this is wrong, but what I am saying is that you need to take the time to build out systems that will get things done completely and most accurately the first time.

Most loan officers want to put the cart before the horse. They go into the business for the wrong reasons. They know someone who is doing very well financially, and they want the riches of the business. The problem is they are chasing someone else's dream.

Running in a lane that was created for someone else never works in the long term. Generally, after failing, these same loan officers go on to their next adventure.

The second word is **excuses**. I must thank Omega Psi Phi, Fraternity Inc. for making sure I never use this word and my family never uses this word. The definition of an excuse is attempt to lessen the blame attaching to (a fault or offense); seek to defend or justify.

Mortgage loan officers! Stop blaming your team (processors, assistants, underwriters, and closers) the buck stops with you. You are the boss, and it is your responsibility to make sure that your business runs smoothly.

Say this every morning when you wake up until you stop making excuses when things don't go your way:

> ***Excuses are the tools of incompetence,***
> ***that build monuments of nothingness,***
> ***and those who so often use them***
> ***rarely accomplish anything.***

Loan officers always ask me this question: "How should I run my business?" Todd Duncan told me about 25 years ago to run your mortgage business like a doctor's office. You have a mortgage practice.

I'm just truly understanding the significance of this statement. Think about it this way, when you get to your doctor's office you must have an appointment. You get checked in and most of your time is with the nurses and other staff. The Doctor comes in for about 5 minutes, asks you a few questions and makes his/her diagnosis.

If you don't have an appointment, you will stay all day. You can't just call your doctor anytime and get them on the phone, you will most likely have to leave a message. You can ask your doctor to make a house call or meet you at your office.

I have watched loan officers get up and go out to meet with realtors to do credit counseling for hours and then complain about having too much work to do. I have seen many loan officers lose good deals because their clients feel neglected by them.

You must work by appointment only. Time yourself on your non-income producing activity, and follow a set schedule. You set your schedule, time blocks, and appointments.

I have been trained with the best mortgage coaches and they all say the same thing about time blocking. You must commit to certain activities daily.

Monday is a great day to reach out realtors and other referral partners. Tuesday is a good day to reach out to active clients under contract, buyers, and listing agents. Wednesday/Thursday I reach to all pre-approvals to make sure that all is well with them and to let them know who to contact over the weekend if I'm not available. Friday is my day, I handle my personal and family business as well as other things for myself.

Loan Officers should also meet with referral partners weekly, have family time, gym time, spiritual/ministry time, and etc. Your goal is to have all of your weekly and monthly activities on your calendar. You also need an accountability partner or coach/mentor to make sure you stay on the course.

I fall behind some weeks, so I use Friday to make sure that I catch up. Remember if there is something you don't have time for, it should never be calling referral partners, active clients under contract, and pre-approvals. This is the 93 octane your car needs to run. If I'm going to miss something in a week it will be my credit challenged clients or those who have not completed my application link. These are my 87 octane clients who can keep me going or cause engine/system problems for my team.

Most loans get denied because of two reasons. Either some credit is not good enough to get loan approval or the number one reason is that most loans get denied because of the borrowers DTI(Debt to Income Ratio).

The four loan programs FHA, Rural Housing, Conventional, and VA financing all use a variation of the DTI rule. And with the federal government defining what a Qualified Mortgage (QM) it makes it more difficult to try to push the envelope.

Almost anyone with a pulse could get approved for financing before the mortgage meltdown of 2008. After the government had to bail out most of our financial institutions and some failed, we finally got mortgage financing laws and rules.

I could never understand why we did not have these rules in the first place. Can you say greed? It was greed from the corporations, Wall Street, banks, mortgage companies, and the consumers. That is right! We all played a role in the mortgage collapse.

A week prior to writing this chapter in May 2023, I received a call from a young lady who was crying on the phone. She had been pre-qualified by a lender who did not verify her information or let an underwriter verify her information to make sure she would get approved. This does not sound like much, but this young lady had moved out of her apartment was living in a hotel and had all her belongings in a U-Haul truck. I tried to help her but she was still determined to believe that the other lender would get her closed. After 3-4 delayed closings the seller released her contract, and she gave up. I called her a couple of times, but her voicemail is full and she has not returned my calls.

How could this person who did this too this young lady sleep at night? I don't want to believe that this was intentional, and I understand that fact that our business is comprised of most loan officers are paid on commission only. Therefore, they try to make every loan work.

We need to focus on helping people. We can't put our personal needs in front of our client's needs. I got off track in business a few times which caused me to try to help people I knew were not ready to buy a home. I needed the commission, so I tried to force the issue. Both times caused my team a lot of stress, bad customer and realtor reviews, and I lost some good business relationships.

I have learned that if I focus on helping people (servant leader) then God can focus on helping me and taking care of my needs.

Let me tell you what changed me. The first time was about 29 years ago, and I gave a client letter of pre-qualification to purchase a home. The loan was eventually approved and closed but it had delays for almost a month. This was way before cell phones, but my pager and office phone never stopped ringing. I soon realized that my loan was delaying about 6 other sales and purchases.

My one little loan was affecting 3 sellers, 3 buyers, and 6 real estate agents. That is a total of 12 families involved in this one little transaction. In my mind I was convinced that I was just trying to help my borrower. Once I looked back on the entire situation, I could not answer the question of whether I was trying to look out for the interests of my borrower or myself.

The bottom line is I gave this client a letter without fully qualifying her. I was just happy to have a loan. Some of these folks had threatened my life, were coming by my job, and were threatening to come to my home. They asked me could they come stay with me until I got this loan closed.

I prayed and asked God to get me out of the mess I had made and I promised to never do it again. This is one of my superpowers. I use empathy at a high level. My wife always jokes with me because she says I use my superpower with strangers but always seem to hold her accountable. She is always held at a higher standard. I guess it is some truth in the old saying that we normally hurt the folks that are too closest to us. The second time I did a letter of pre-qualification was in 2007-2008 when the mortgage business was struggling. I had 3 mortgage offices with leases, mortgages, employees, and a whole lot of debt. I also owned a construction company that was developing a subdivision and had about six spec homes that were built with no buyers in sight. Can you say underwater? My bills outweighed my assets, and I had no way out. The third time I gave a client a pre-qualification letter was in 2014. I gave a life time client a letter of pre-qualification before I ran his file through AUS (Automated Underwriting) . His loan was not initially approved, and it took me some time to get his credit report updated. The seller's agent filed a complaint with the state of Virginia, and they conducted an investigation. Because they found that I had given him an approval letter 2 weeks before he got loan approval that I had committed a violation.

The fine was five thousand dollars. I said from that point on that no one gets an approval letter unless I have all of their loan documents, AUS approval, or approval from my underwriter. In the mortgage business, you cannot afford to lose your license. I needed my license to support myself and my family. I purposed myself to be thorough about doing any approval letters.

The moral of this chapter is that with technology and support you don't have to take risks which can be detrimental to people livelihoods and subsequently threaten your licensing. We have AUS (Automated Underwriting) , ways to verify employment and people to review tax returns and calculate income. We have companies who can fix a credit reports in days. They can tell your client what to pay to improve their credit scores. If you are mastering the mortgage programs, learn how to read credit reports accurately, and calculate income correctly, then you will be a good loan officer.

Never give your opinion (pre-qualification letter), work with the facts. Make sure that the loan is approved and will close the way you have structured it from the beginning. You should know your mortgage guidelines like you know your name. The top loan officers make as much doctors and lawyers. My mentor, Todd Duncan, always told me to run my business like a doctor's office. I want to get paid like a doctor. Why would I not take the time to make sure that I do my job right the first time?I know Doctors make mistakes too, but look at how much schooling and training they compete successfully before earning the title of Medical Doctor.

If you master the mortgage programs and become at least a 'purple belt' at qualifying your clients and understanding credit you will be better than 95% of the loan officers out there today.

Make sure you have access to the guidelines to know what is acceptable because each loan program has different requirements. FHA and VA are more lenient on credit than your USDA and Conventional programs. Also, the AUS findings will tell you everything that is needed for your loan. Did you know that in 2023 most loan officers still don't read the findings? I had a loan officer tell me the other day that she was too busy to read the findings. You can be very busy, but not productive. If you have a lot of chaos and disorganization, you are busy in a bad way. I see people working seven days a week, not having a good home life and not making enough money to take care of themselves or their families. Your business should run on systems not on needs and wants. This is when we get ourselves in trouble. This is when we try to put the 87-octane gas in a car that needs 93 octane.

If you work with a system and master the entire loan process to become a Complete Loan Officer, you will never look for business again. I had a meeting with some of my loan officers last week and one of them has been struggling for years, and I mean years. He has over 20 years in the business and does not close loans consistently. He tells me that he knows he is a great Loan Officer. He has not mastered the mortgage programs, but he is good at them and the mortgage process.

He has two big problems that will continue to keep him from success. He has a bad attitude (bad energy) most of the time and he does not have empathy for his clients. He says he does, but he is more concerned with his needs first. Then he considers the needs of his clients or co-workers. As I continue to learn more about myself, God's is helping me to help others. This thing called life is a journey not a race.

Chapter Five:
Be Honest With Yourself

I'm in a much better place at 54 than I was about 30 years ago when this loan officer journey began. I have been at the top of the mountain and at the bottom of the valley. I can honestly say that I have had way more good days than bad days. My family life is flourishing. I have two grandchildren and all my children are grown. I have made some bad business decisions both in my construction and mortgage business in the past. I have earned a good amount of money and I have also wasted money on bad investments (flip houses/new construction homes) with the wrong partners and no systems in place.

I have managed to make some great accomplishments in my life with no real plan. I realize that by not having a plan, I was setting myself up for failure. I thank God that he brought Eboni into my life to be both my wife and business partner. She reminds me of Father in the way she speaks to people, and she doesn't take nonsense from anyone. She is my Why.

The more we talk and the more she lets me inside of her world I realize how good my life has been. Eboni has been through a lot in all of her years. I know one of her superpowers is to help others reach their dreams. She has been encouraging me for almost thirteen years. She helped me organize a construction business that I initially opened in 2014. This is the second time I have opened a construction company.

My wife helped me get my mortgage business back on track. She continues to help me be myself and bring out the best in me. Before I met Eboni, I would not tell people how I really felt. I would bottle up my emotions until I exploded. Most of the time on the wrong people. She helped me channel my discerning energy to stop trusting the wrong people.

As Eboni would say to me," it is time to 'cut their nuts". She does not judge people she just keeps her circle small. It is hard to do this while trying to build a business, but I'm learning that every business relationship does not have to be a friendship and every friendship does not have to result in doing business together. Some will consist of both, but it is okay to have friends and business associates separate and apart from each other. In fact, it is better that way because I never want to lose true friends. Money has a way of causing problems in your relationships if ventures ever go wrong.

Eboni has helped me to spend more time reading and listening to audio books than I would have ever imagined. I literally have not been wanting to learn anything that would not make me money. I did not spend a lot of time reading the word or reading self-improvement books. I now read or listen to any book that piques my interest or comes highly recommended by a friend or mentor. I'm seeking more information about theology school, and I love mentoring and helping people maximize their potential in life. I'm becoming what God has created me to be. I'm becoming a life, spiritual, and business coach all in one person. I used to think that

I could only coach mortgage professionals but realize that everyone needs God and mentors in their life.

I'm not sure if I will be mentoring children or teenagers at this time, but I love talking to people who are trying make sense of this thing called life. I always try to use my superpower of empathy to feel what someone else is feeling whether that is pain or joy. I want to continue to learn more about the creator, so that I can use my superpower of empathy to discern what God has for my purpose on this earth. I heard my mentor Myron Golden say that we need to slow down and read the bible so we can hear what God is saying to us. I realize that we have to first slow down in life to read the bible to hear what God is saying.

On May 24, 2023, I woke to write this chapter at 2am. I was inspired by a book that am reading in my Morning Meet-up with David Shands entitled, "You owe You" by Eric Thomas. I pondered about two things. What is my superpower? And why did I spend those three hours watching basketball when I have not finished my book?

Myron Golden, David Shands, and Eric Thomas have shown me some great things over the last few months. I have been blessed to make good money and have nice things, but I was not doing it while becoming financially free. How can I reach my full potential if I have to worry about paying bills and taking care of my family? I had been in this before and it did not feel good and here I'm again at this same crossroad. More debt than income and still trying to help everyone else. That is a part of that superpower because God is allowing me to make enough income to pay my bills and take care of my family. I could have been debt free 10 times over. I make impulsive decisions sometimes that get me in more debt.

In Myron Golden in his book "From the Trash Man to the Cash Man" talks about the financial management system to help you become rich. I have finally started taking a close look at my finances to work towards financial freedom. I am committed to working towards becoming a better tither. I won't purchase anything unless it makes more money than it costs monthly. I mean rental property that pays for itself or other investments. I'm not buying a boat unless another asset can pay for it. I won't purchase any more cars unless we have a business need for the construction company. I will work to pay off all the bills I have now that are weighing me down both physically and mentally. I don't need any more baggage.

I have learned two vitally important concepts from both Myron Golden and Eric Thomas. Myron always says that if you lie to yourself you will lie to anybody. I have been lying to myself for years. Telling myself that I'm doing my best. That is a lie. I have been telling myself that I needed those name brand expensive shoes, clothes, cars, and a boat. I've have said, "You deserve these things because you work so hard." The working hard part is the truth, but, I purchased these items with cash that was needed for other more expedient things. I have used money that should have gone to paying off high interest debt, like my credit cards.

I would spend money from houses I was building before I sold them. That is how I convinced myself to purchase a sports car at 52 years old. My wife calls my car my other *woman*. (Thanks, Eboni, for naming my car a girl.)

After the 5-year layoff from building homes I tried to jump right back on the horse and it was horrible. I vowed to never build another house in 2020. The first two houses we built with two partners cost me more money out of pocket than I made. I took a big loss. I used my savings to pay off credits and am still paying off a cabinet company and Lowes while I finish this book. I had bad partners, sub-contractors, private loans, and no plans.

My new business partner is making waves. She has a definitive plan that includes me and my services. She has put a plan in place that is no nonsense, and it works. She *'cut everyone's nuts'* including mine.

Now that business is thriving, I want to help the working class get attainable housing because being a MLO I see the struggles with finding homes they can afford to purchase. I heard of a State Trooper not being able to purchase a home in the area because of the cost of high real estate. We must do better to help the folks that take care of this country. I realize that overextending myself both financially and personally would never allow me to reach my full potential. If you need to figure out what your superpower is then slow down so God can show it to you. If you already know what your superpower is then embrace it. Work today freeing yourself so that you can embrace it. I'm completely comfortable in being the real me (thanks Eric Thomas) It's only then that I can maximize my full potential. I will start to give my gift to as many people as I can help.

What is realize is that financial freedom comes to you when you put your focus into maximizing your God-given gifts and giving them freely to others. It totally blows my mind when I think about what God does for his children.   As He continues to bless me, I have to be more responsible with my finances. I will hold myself accountable and invest wisely. More assets and no liabilities is the goal for 2023 and beyond!

Chapter Six:
Fulfilling Your God-Given Purpose

I would like to give a special thanks to the Blandford Community and the City of Petersburg. We are a little city and small community, but I know that without my humble beginnings that this life journey would not be so sweet. I would like to thank my parents and mentors along the journey. I would like to thank my wife Eboni Nunnally and my children and grandchildren. I would like to thank my family, friends, and fraternity brothers. I would like to thank my alma mater Old Dominion University.

Owners of New American Funding. Thanks Patty and Rick for showing me how a successful mortgage company can be run. You have taken my passion for helping the underserved to a level that I could not even dream of. We are about 5k strong and the level of service and commitment to excellence at NAF is second to none. I wish I had mentors like you when I first opened my mortgage and construction businesses the late 1990's and early 2000's. The irony of it all was that I would not have understood what to do at that time even if you showed me. I was not ready to be a successful entrepreneur at the levels that I dreamed about.

God has always allowed me to see into my future and what it looks like as I follow Him without wavering. Despite my own shortfalls, He continues to be faithful. My fraternity has taught me over these last 34 years that we must "See it Through" and no "Excuses" failing is not an option. I hope that this book helps any loan officers struggling with their careers and other people struggling with life.

God created us to do something to glorify his kingdom and it is our job to figure out what that is. If you walk in what God has created you to do it will come easy and he has already blessed it. Stop going in the direction that you want to and follow God.

As the Business Bishop Wayne Malcolm would say, **"Know your purpose/why and then become the King /Queen of it."**

My Pastor Barbara Salley preached a sermon a few months ago and stuck with me for life. She said, "Strong Faith, Strong Finish."

That is my goal until God calls me home. I feel strongly that finding a good church home is imperative. Bishop Salley and Pastor Salley have made this journey move forward in a positive direction. I did not know how much I needed that spiritual mentorship until now. My relationship with God and my Church here in Maryland has given me a peace that I cannot understand.

When I lost my earthly father in 2014, I lost my best friend in the world. My father was such an important person in my life for for almost 45 years. He was my role model and I wanted to make him proud. Though nothing can replace him, God sent me Eboni Nunnally to fill the void that was left inside of me when he died. He also gave me a great home church with leaders whose fifty year relationship is an example for me. I want to give Eboni the real me that God created.

In hindsight that I was mature enough to stay on this journey twenty years ago. God had a different plan for my life. The peaks and valleys, highs and the lows, have made me who I'm today. Thank you, God!

Before we look more into mastering the MLO Pyramid, I want to discuss the Pyramid of a Complete Believer. The foundation of this pyramid begins with your spiritual walk with the Creator.

"Train a child up in the way he should go, and he should not depart from it." (Proverbs 22:6).

I was introduced to the Church and our Lord and Savior Jesus Christ at a very young age. It was learned behavior from my grandparents and parents. I did not truly know God for myself.

As I got older and became a young adult I began to question some of the teachings from my childhood. My faith has been tested many times with life's trials and tribulations. I'm learning to lean on God and not my own understanding in this life journey.

Put all of your trust in Him. Without any uncertainty, He will show you if this profession is part of His plan for your life. He will never let you down. Study his word, meditate, and find a spiritual coach/mentor.

The second level of the pyramid is Vision/Purpose. You must understand why you do what you do. You should start seeing that this is what God created you to do. I must study to master my craft. You need to become the 'King of your Thing', as Bishop Wayne Malcolm would say.

The next level of the pyramid should be Commitment and Execution. You can have strong faith, but you must still work. As you build your team your goal should be to become a servant leader. I always try to look back at Jesus Christ to know that all great leaders should focus on serving.

This means building your team and the culture of your business around helping others. You should always have a team first approach to your business. There is no 'I' in team. As your team begins to work well together you will see your legacy begin. This is where mastery happens. Once you get mastery or your 'black belt' in all levels of the Pyramid of a Complete Loan Officer and the Pyramid of a Complete Believer, life will become that much sweeter.

Chapter Seven:
Understanding the Pyramid of the Complete Mortgage Loan Officer(MLO)

To become a Complete MLO, you must have three main systems in Place. You must have a POP (Perfect Origination System), PLP(, and Perfect Loan Process)PCP(Perfect Closing Process).

We will start with the POP (Perfect Origination System). The MLO's main job in the business is to generate loans. I feel that the MLO should work on mastering two parts of the pyramid first. Essential Knowledge and Marketing will be the key components in building a successful business.

You must study daily to work towards becoming a 'black belt/master' in the POP system. Once you build out your POP system it will be like fuel to a car. The key is making sure you are not putting 87 octane gas in a car built to run on 93 octane gasoline. If you are good at starting fires, creating chaos, and not understanding or mastering loan products, then this is not for you. I am talking to the MLOs who want to operate on a higher level. Leads can be generated in several different ways. Some MLO'S buy leads, run ads, send out mailers, and even run radio and television commercials. Lately, social media has also been a good way to generate leads; there is nothing wrong with this approach. I prefer relationship building, referral partners (realtors, builders, CPA, and financial advisors) who I can connect with, and form teams. I refer them to clients, and they do the same. I prefer working with people that I like and know personally. As my mentor would say, I prefer the rifle approach versus the shotgun approach. I identify my target, qualify them, aim and shoot. Hopefully I hit a bullseye. I'm at my best when I'm seen as a partner, mortgage expert, trusted advisor or mortgage certified planner. You get the point. When AJ3 speaks, people listen. Some realtors are dictators and unethical. I stay far away from these people no matter how much business they could possibly generate. My goal is to always make sure that any potential client gets special treatment from my team.

It begins with me. When I get a referral, I make the initial introduction. When I connect with a new realtor, I spend the time getting to know them personally. I want to make sure we are a good fit. I don't discuss mortgage programs unless asked and I don't discuss the company who I'm employed with. My goal is to know what the referral partner is all about. I want to know their goals, about their family and their interests. After I take the time to vet them on a more personal level, I then discuss what lenders they work with. I find out what they like about their current lender and what could be done better. I always try to meet at a neutral location. It is important for me to get them out of the office and for me to get out of the office so I can have their undivided attention. I consider this our first date. We can both leave the meeting deciding if this is a relationship worth pursuing. If we have to meet at our office or there office I will select the conference room for the meeting. I turn off my cell phone and ask them to do the same.

I can say that I have had referral partners who did not want to work with me and vice versa. If they don't want to work with me then I see it as their loss. I know that my team is the best. If you don't feel that way about yourself and your team, then we have work to do. Every client should feel like you are their mortgage concierge. My team knows that whether a potential client is approved, has credit challenges, or very little income, we will try to help them.

In my career I have done loans north of a million dollars and loans south of fifty thousand.

We give out gifts to our clients at pre-approval (once all documents are received), ratified contract, and at/or after closing. All clients get weekly follow-up phone calls and these gifts. If a client does not complete my application link or has not provided necessary information to complete the approval process, then they get weekly emails and phone calls. I want to make sure they are still interested in moving forward and if they need help with any part of the process. If they need me to input their information for loan application, then my team will make that happen. If they need to come by the office to drop off documents or have us meet them, we make this happen. I want to add that you should never put your safety in danger. My realtor partners are great at assisting with this. Remember we are a team.

If we have clients with credit challenges, we provide them with a copy of their credit report and a detailed game plan of what they must do to move forward. Sometimes it takes years and sometimes clients must file bankruptcy. If they owe more than their annual salary it is more than likely that these bills can never be paid off. I normally give the client the option of a referral to a credit expert or some choice to work on their own credit. I always clear it with my realtor partner before I make any recommendations. I used to work on client's credit for them, but this is very time-consuming and not a good use of your time.

To stay organized every potential client is entered into my CRM (Customer Relationship Management). I believe it is vital to categorize and give task to every client who comes your way. If they take the time to call me and are sincere about home ownership, then we want to help. I have learned to give more priority to my clients preapproved and under contract to make sure we keep and earn their business. All of my clients are equally important to my team we just understand that a client under contract needing to close in 15-30 days takes precedence over a client coming out of a bankruptcy looking to purchase next year. I use different categories to log my clients. All clients are logged as:

1.   *Pre-approved*

2.   *NMI (Need more information)*

3.   *GRFH (Getting Ready for Home).*

I used to call my GRFH clients credit counseling, but it sounded negative. I changed the label to GRFH to make preparation for calling these clients more palatable and positive. I never want to feel as if I'm wasting time with people, and I never want my clients to feel that they are wasting their time seeking to become homeowners. You should always have a separate CRM from your employer. Remember you are the boss. What happens if your company lays you off? Do you think they will export your CRM to you and stop calling on your clients? They will never stop contacting your clients. That is why I make sure that my referral partners and my clients know that they work with AJ3, Your Mortgage QB Team. They understand that I own this business and that my employer is the tool we use to help them.

I recommend all MLO's to focus on becoming a servant leader. Join the Realtor Association in your city or town. Join organizations like NAREB, VAREB, Chamber of Commerce, etc. Become active in civic organizations and your church. Teach financial literacy to people and children. The lack of knowledge is really hurting black and brown people.

I believe in creating Generational Wealth. I know that real estate ownership is the foundation for that to happen. I used to say that I wanted to make sure that my next generation was good. After listening to Bishop Wayne Malcolm speak on Generational Wealth, I want to make sure that 4 generations are good, that is 200 years of my family.

Chapter Eight:
Developing The Perfect Loan Process

Now that you are well on your way to mastering the Essential Knowledge and Marketing part of the pyramid, we can focus on creating and building our next system. This is the second system but is just as important as the first. This system is the PLP (Perfect Loan Process). This part of the system covers the point in time when the loan officer gets the contract and passes the baton to their loan officer assistant. I learned this concept from Loan Toolbox and Tim Braheem. I have to thank my mentors, Craig Stent and Mike Pearson of Apex Home Loans for reintroducing this system to me. It has changed my life.

This system on my team involves five people. They are my team lead/MLO assistant, setup person, processor, underwriter, and closer. The team lead and processor work directly for my team and the others work for the company. The great thing about my company is that they have a great system and work ethic that allows we to integrate my system into their process flow.

My parent company is a Ferrari or better yet a private jet. They make things happen and give me all the tools I need to service my clients. When I give a file to my team lead the only thing, I have to do is lock in the interest rate and go to closing. They make sure that everything else is handled. They make detailed notes on what I'm doing and they communicate with my team on both my expectations and the referral partner and clients' expectations. We all agree that we will be able to meet you and exceed those goals.

What I pride myself on is turning in a complete file. I make sure that that the agents and borrowers know who my processor and team lead are and that they will be taking over the process from that point. I make sure to let them know that both my team lead and processor are very knowledgeable and that they are in good hands. I always let them know that these ladies keep me on track.

I also let them know that I will be checking in with them weekly, but any questions about the documents needed for their loan should be directed to my team. If they have questions about the payment or cash to close, then they come to me. If they call or email me about questions pertaining to documents with their loan, I kindly refer them back to my team. There are two main reasons I do this. One: I need to stay in my lane and focus on getting more business and referral partners. I have to commit to and execute my time management system. Two: I must ensure that my realtors, clients, and team know I have total confidence in their abilities. That means I have to delegate duties. I don't know what the team has requested, I could misspeak and cause confusion for us all.

Am I my MLO keeper? My team lead and processor would say yes, I am. They are really a great support system. I love and appreciate all that they do for me. They have stayed up really late to make sure my sure that my Closing Disclosure (CD) is delivered electronically to the client so that we can close on time.

This CD must be delivered 3 business days before the scheduled closing. We submit the closing disclosure while we are working on getting the loan submitted for authorization to close. I have seen my loan processor send out the CD at 11pm to make sure it is dated on the day that we need in order to close on time. My team even sends out pre-approvals for me on the weekends when I'm on vacation.

You'd better not mess with my team if you don't want to deal with AJ3 directly! For the loan officers who take their teams for granted and are very negative in communication, I suggest that you be a loan officer assistant, processor, underwriter, or closer for a few days. Walk in their shoes and you will truly appreciate the efforts put into making your team successful.

Show your team love both financially and through other methods of appreciation. I give gifts, bonuses, team building days (paid time off for fun activities) as well as other perks. They are the life blood of your organization. Treat them right! Now that I have a great team lead and processor, I appreciate them every day. I Thank God for them both. I'm not saying that we are perfect because I know we are not. We all make mistakes daily, but we learn from our mistakes. Our systems help us avoid the big mistakes that can't be fixed.

I had been about 10 years in the business and my processor called me from a pay phone and told me she was not coming back. She loves me but she could not work with our operations manager. I had about 30 files in processing with no processor. I was threatened daily that all my loans were sitting and going past the closing date. I tried to process them and failed. I was putting the wrong documents in other files, and I was literally losing my mind. I said Lord this job isn't for me. Finally, I calmed down and started working on the loans one at a time. Things started moving and loans were closing. I made a mental note that this would never happen to me again. I learned how to process files and underwrite files from that day forward. I keep underwriting manuals on my laptop and in my bookshelves. I review the conditions. I can call the underwriter to question conditions and have even called HUD and VA to discuss some concerns with guidelines. I mean like borrower doesn't qualify, wrong income, wrong program, not enough eligibility as a veteran and a slew of other problems that could be avoided with the attention to detail that comes with being organized and having a smoothly running, competent team.

I'm a servant leader, I follow God, so I forgive people and try to remain humble in my daily walk. We keep it simple when we make mistakes. This is our motto–Problem, Solution, Next Task. If a problem happens more then once we need to change our system to make sure that it does not happen again. We are a work in progress, and we have the same common goal to give excellent customer service so that our referral partners and borrowers become customers for life.

Our company sends out weekly milestone reports to all parties. My team lead sends out weekly status reports and I try to send out weekly video status reports. We try to get all loans cleared to close in 14 business days no matter what the closing date is on the contract. We go over payments and cash to close 3 days before closing in most cases. We want to make sure the client is comfortable with the monthly payments and cash to close. No one likes surprises at the closing table. You will lose your referral partners and gain a bad reputation. We try to attend all closings when possible, because, if there is something wrong it can be corrected quickly. I have learned that if you are not at the closing and there is a problem you will be blamed. Like my good friend Guy Allen (Realtor/President of our NAREB) says, if you are not at the table you are probably on the menu.

Make sure that your PLP system is scalable and that you meet with your team weekly after implementation. After your system is running smoothly you can move meetings back to bi-weekly or monthly. Always value the opinions of your processor and team lead. Remember, I'm only a purple belt at processing and no belt at organizational skills, so I thank God that my team lead and processor are both black belts.

After a successful closing is when the work truly begins. Did you receive a excellent on your customer survey. If not, reach out to the realtors and clients to see what you could have done better. Make sure you share this information with your team. If you see something more than once remember to change your POP or PLP systems. I had to change my POP system twice while writing this book. At first, I would email and not call my pre-approvals, need more information and get ready for home ownership clients. I would call my pre-approvals sometimes and email my need more information clients. What I learned was eye opening. I lost 3 clients in two months. They were under contract or had closed on their new homes. One client in particular asked me if she could tell me why she went with another lender. She said," Mr. Nunnally I really liked you and you were very knowledgeable in what you told me to do. I just felt like I needed someone more attentive to my needs. Sometimes I felt that you were too busy to assist me. I really feel bad for sharing this with you." Another client changed realtors and was convinced to go with the realtor lender. I never introduced myself to the client's new realtor. Both of these losses could have been prevented if I had operated under my POP system. I still sent these clients closing gifts because it was not their fault that they closed with other lenders, it was my fault.

Remember I'm the boss. I am the CEO of Me. You'd better believe that my POP system has me making calls and leaving messages instead of sending emails. I have since acquired 2 new clients and saved a couple of deals.

I recently finished a few books that have really blessed my business. I recommend "The E-Myth Revisited" by Michael E. Gerber, " Who Not How" and "The Gap and the Gain" both by Dan Sullivan and Dr. Benjamin Hardy, and "Trash Man to Cash man' by Myron Golden.

I listen to audio books, read books, write, and study successful entrepreneurs on you-tube daily. The great thing about 2023 is if you want to learn something or listen to like-minded people in your industry to you can find them instantly and usually free of charge, just a sacrifice of your time.

Chapter Nine:
Developing The Perfect Closing Process

The final system is the PPCP (Perfect Post Closing Process). If you are a Certified Mortgage Planner and you want to manage your client's mortgage for life, then you must have a good Customer Relationship Management System to keep track of your customers and connections in a timely fashion. Your CRM will notify you when it's time to get in touch with them to follow up.

We recommend calling about 2 weeks after closing to do a wellness check. You should also set alerts on your CRM to notify you when your client's interest rate can be lowered from .50-1%. We do annual mortgage reviews, and we send out quarterly newsletters, birthday cards, anniversary cards, and our company co-brands us and the agents on quarterly mortgage statements. I told you that my company is amazing. We service about 97% of our loans. If you master the Essential Knowledge and Marketing part of the Pyramid of a Complete Loan Officer and Build your team out with people who have a 'purple belt' working on a 'black belt' in operations and team building, then you are well on your way to legacy building.

Remember that you will have two pyramids, one for work and one for your personal life. You must master them both to get the top of the Pyramid Legacy-financial freedom and generational wealth creation.

Chapter Ten:
Mastering Mortgage Product Knowledge & Qualifying Clients

Most businesses fail in the first 3-5 years. They don't fail because of not having a great idea. They fail because they don't have a great plan or preparation for the capital needed to keep going though the start-up phase. Most loan officers fail because of the same reason.

They pass the test, get licensed and sponsored by a company and are off and running. They know of someone or have heard that MLO's make a lot of money which is very true for the top 10% of the loan officers in the country. Even then, the market dictates the peaks and valleys of your success.

I mean when the interest rates are higher less people seem compelled to refinance or sell their home and purchase another home. First Time Home Buyers are confused because they get conflicting information from the media, co-workers, family members, and friends.

I have been in the mortgage industry for almost 31 years. I have definitely seen my share of peaks and valleys. I recommend that you have at least l year reserves for all your expenses when you're starting off in this business. Try to obtain a salaried position, or get a personal loan or line of credit for start up and survivor costs. If you can't feed your family and pay your bills it will be almost impossible for you to follow your plan, concentrate on learning, and giving your business 100% of you to learn.

I want to recommend that you spend your initial days, months, and years mastering three things in the mortgage process. The first is product knowledge, second is understating how to read and improve a credit report (score) and third is understanding how to calculate income correctly.

Product knowledge is where most MLO's lack interest. You must learn while you earn. Remember knowledge is the foundation of the Pyramid of a Complete Loan Officer. I know that it is a lot of information to retain, and the industry is constantly changing and evolving, but, if you master the four basic loan programs you will be able to learn any program. I always try to keep things simple.

It is just like in grade school we all started with basic math. Imagine if we had to learn calculus or geometry in first grade or kindergarten. It would be rough on our children, the teachers, and the parents. I probably would still be in elementary school.

While there are hundreds and maybe even thousands of mortgage loan products, most clients receive one of these four loans. They either get a conventional (Private Sector), FHA (Insured by Federal Government), VA (Guaranteed by the Federal Government), or USDA (Guaranteed by the Federal Government) loan. So, if you master these four programs you will have your foundation solid for your pyramid.

When I get a new lead, I have a list of questions that I ask, and I let them tell me their goals. This helps me start to eliminate the programs that they are not eligible for. For example, if they have never served in the military then we can't consider a VA Loan. This loan program is only for veterans or possible survivor spouses of veterans. Second, if they want to live in the city then I know that they are not eligible for USDA (Rural Housing) financing. This type of loan is only allowed in rural areas. Also, if they tell me that their salary is above the median income then USDA is probably out because they have income limits. This helps me head in the right direction to determine the best program for the client. If they tell me that they will not be occupying the property (investment property) or that it will be a second home, then this will eliminate all programs except conventional financing. FHA, VA, and USDA financing is only allowed on properties that our clients will occupy as their primary residence.

I also have the client complete the loan application and get authorization to run their credit. I try not to discuss to much information before we determine what their credit score is and I review their complete tri-merge report. Some companies only do a soft pull to pre-qualify a client and this is risky. I prefer doing a tri-merge report to make sure that there is nothing out there that could change the decision on the loan. I only issue pre-approval or commitment letters for my clients. We are in a very competitive market where sellers are receiving multiple offers in highly desired areas and some cash offers. Some of these offers are well above the asking price of these homes. If you are only giving out pre-qualified letters, then you are putting your clients at a big disadvantage in the market.

Once you run the credit report and have the credit score you can determine whether your client will need to go Conventional or FHA. Normally if the client's score is 640 or below and they are putting down 3.5%-5% then I would recommend FHA for the financing. Your interest rate with most programs is based on your credit score. The higher the credit score the lower the rate and the cost for the interest rate. The benefit of FHA is that the MIP (Mortgage Insurance Premium) is not based primarily off of your credit score. That means that the MIP paid for by a person with a 580- 850 credit score would be the same.

I know that does not seem fair and it is not. Remember that the Federal Government created the FHA loan program to assist families who had less income, assets, and not perfect credit. I feel like it was created to help the underserved. FHA allows lower credit scores, less time elapse of derogatory credit (example collections, foreclosures, and bankruptcies), higher debt to income ratios with housing and other liabilities.

If you have higher credit scores and are putting down a 10-20% downpayment then I would always recommend Conventional Financing. Conventional Financing rewards excellent credit with lower rates and if you are putting down between 3%-19% you will be paying PMI (Private Mortgage Insurance) . This insurance protects the lender if you default. It does not benefit your borrower at all except allowing them to purchase a home with less than 20% down payment. The benefit of conventional financing is that if you have excellent credit your PMI will be a lot cheaper than FHA.

Also, if you are putting down a 20% down payment your risk levels fall below the limit, so you are not required to pay mortgage insurance. FHA will still charge you an mortgage insurance premium. If a client has good credit and a good down payment the only reason, I suggest FHA is because their DTI is above 50%.

If I had to rank these four programs from best to good, then this is my opinion on the number one program is VA, two USDA, three Conventional, and forth is FHA. Remember all of these programs have strengths and weaknesses but are necessary to help families obtain home ownership. By becoming homeowners, we can start to create Generation Wealth for 4 generations of families. As a Certified Mortgage planner, we want to protect and cover 200 years of our families.

A VA loan for veterans is a sweet program. It is always my first recommendation when a client qualifies for this benefit. If you served in the military or are serving in the military to protect this nation you deserve a VIP loan like a VA Loan. I would like to say thank you for your many sacrifices. A VA loan offers zero money down, good interest rate, allows higher debt to income ratios (residual income is also needed to qualify based on family size), credit scores down to 580, and no monthly mortgage insurance.

They do require a Funding Fee (upfront mortgage insurance) that can be financed in your loan. If you are a veteran with disabilities, then the funding fee could be waived. Also, if you had a VA Loan go into foreclosure or own another property with a VA Loan you still could have enough entitlement to purchase another home which must be used as your primary residence.

Remember, VA does not finance investment properties, but they understand that your orders could change, or you could retire and move to another location. Veterans, whether active duty, retired, separated from service (served by not long enough to receive retirement benefits), reservist, and survivor spouses could be eligible for this program.

If the veteran is 100% disabled, he/she could be exempted from the funding fee and real estate taxes. Always check with the state, city, and county to see if the 100% disabled veteran is eligible for exemption from real estate taxes. This is up to the locality to offer this service. Know your guidelines and where to look to get the correct answers. The VA Loan guidelines are online for you to download and study.

My second choice would be a USDA (Rural Housing, Rural Development) loan. This loan is very similar to a VA Loan. It has zero down payment, credit scores as low as 620, minimal mortgage insurance upfront and monthly. The negatives of this program are that it can only be used in certain areas. You must run the property address through a geographic census map to see if it is eligible. When I started 31 years ago, we did not have a computer software program to determine if a property was eligible, we had actual maps with lines drawn and we had to figure it out. It was tough at times with the properties too close to the line. It could go either way just depending on the day your USDA local representative was having.

HMDA or Home Mortgage Disclosure Act data was not being collected, so discrimination was rampant. HMDA is the federal law that requires lenders to share their mortgage data, so it is possible to better determine and dismantle credit discrimination practices. This program looks at the median income for a family to determine eligibility. It also offers a subsidized program that will pay part of your mortgage monthly to help you qualify for a home. This is set up to help the underserved who are below the income median. I think this is a great way to break the poverty cycle and help families build generational wealth.

Like my college professor would always say there is no such thing as a free meal. The part of the payment that the federal government pays to you each month is repaid once you sell the property. Don't look at the cup as half empty but look at it half full. If the government does not pay part of your payment, you would not have been able to purchase a home. If you stay in the home for 20-30 years and pay it off the property could be worth hundreds of thousands of dollars. You would have received a tax benefit (speak to a Tax Professional) and you will have a good amount of equity. If you were renting all this time.

In conclusion, becoming a Mortgage Loan Officer is a very serious job. We are helping families obtain home ownership which is the largest asset/investment. If we make mistakes or put our clients in harm's way, they could lose everything. With our construction company back in 2010 -2014 we did foreclosure clean outs. It would break my heart when I entered a property and a child's room was still in tact. The family would leave the bed, clothes, toys, etc. like they were coming back. We as mortgage professionals, leaders in the industry, coaches and trainers must do a better job in educating both the

Loan Officers and Consumers. We can't put our personal needs in front of our clients. I must admit that being a African American Mortgage Professional is 10 times harder than it is for Caucasian, Latino, and Asian Mortgage Professionals. This is because most Caucasian, Latino, and Asian realtors will only work with Loan Officers of the same race. African American realtors will work with anyone who closes their deals. I'm very passionate. About moving this needle of home ownership for the underserved.

African Americans are at the bottom of homeownership for the last 50 years. We have not seen much change in this country with homeownership or generational wealth. We must start betting on Black. We are strong people who will continue to prosper no matter what the odds. I just wish we would make more effort in supporting and lifting each other as we climb. I know that some of the problems is that a few bad Loan Officers who happen to be African American have done really bad things. The truth of the matter that bad people do bad things no matter what the race. The problem is that when we commit these crimes it is publicized, scrutinized, and breaking news. When others commit the same crimes or worse crimes, we operate with empathy because of how society has been programmed. For us to make real progress, Black on Black crime must stop in the streets, businesses, and the board rooms. I will take all of us to make real change and silence is not the solution.

What path lies ahead? Whether you're considering a career in the mortgage industry, already immersed in it with varying degrees of success, or thriving financially yet feeling a void in purpose, there's an essential question to ponder: Was I meant to be a Mortgage Loan Officer? In moments of quiet introspection, when both heart and mind are stilled, the answer becomes clear.

I've come to realize that my role as a successful Mortgage Loan Officer constitutes only a small fraction of my true calling. For many years, my pursuit of financial gain overshadowed my deeper purpose. My career spanned building homes and conducting numerous mortgage transactions, all with profitability as the primary goal. However, recent insights from books like David Ramsey's 'The Total Money Makeover' and John Hope Bryant's 'How the Poor Can Save Capitalism' have been enlightening. These books, essential for anyone, especially entrepreneurs and believers in Christ, stress the importance of financial wisdom.

The bondage of debt, a constant worry about bills, shelter, and food, can distract us from our divine purpose. My past few years were marked by unnecessary spending, debt accumulation, and a struggling mortgage business that narrowed my focus to mere survival. However, the clarity of my God-given purpose is emerging, despite such distractions.

Since writing this book, I've made significant changes. I sold my sports car, listed my house for sale, and refocused on growing my mortgage business. Alongside mentoring other Loan Officers and assisting my wife with our construction company, we're developing affordable housing. Our non-profit organization aims to teach financial literacy to both children and adults, helping them with banking, career skills, and housing.

David Ramsey advocates for a debt-free life, investment, enjoyment, and philanthropy. This aligns with the vision God bestowed upon me three decades ago when I entered the mortgage and construction fields. My journey veered off course when I began measuring success against others, shifting from a desire to help the most people to a pursuit of wealth and status symbols. It took me 30 years in this metaphorical wilderness to find my way back.

My book is for believers and non-believers alike, who sense there's more to life than their current path. What is your 'why'? What purpose has God created for you? My mission is to help you discover it, regardless of your profession. In a judgment-free zone, I serve and lead, believing we all have a role in fulfilling God's will.

Becoming the lender, not the borrower, is key to living our purpose. I'm on a journey to debt freedom and plan to educate the younger generation on financial management, instilling the importance of home ownership as a foundation for generational wealth. Despite daunting prospects for African American males, we can defy societal expectations through unity and education. As John Hope Bryant suggests, overcoming a mindset of poverty is crucial. Let's offer our children diverse pathways to success, breaking free from the poverty mindset to realize their full potential."

NOTES

NOTES

NOTES

This is a must-have professional mortgage calculator.

It is just one tool in your arsenal.

Learn how to use this in your day to day operations.

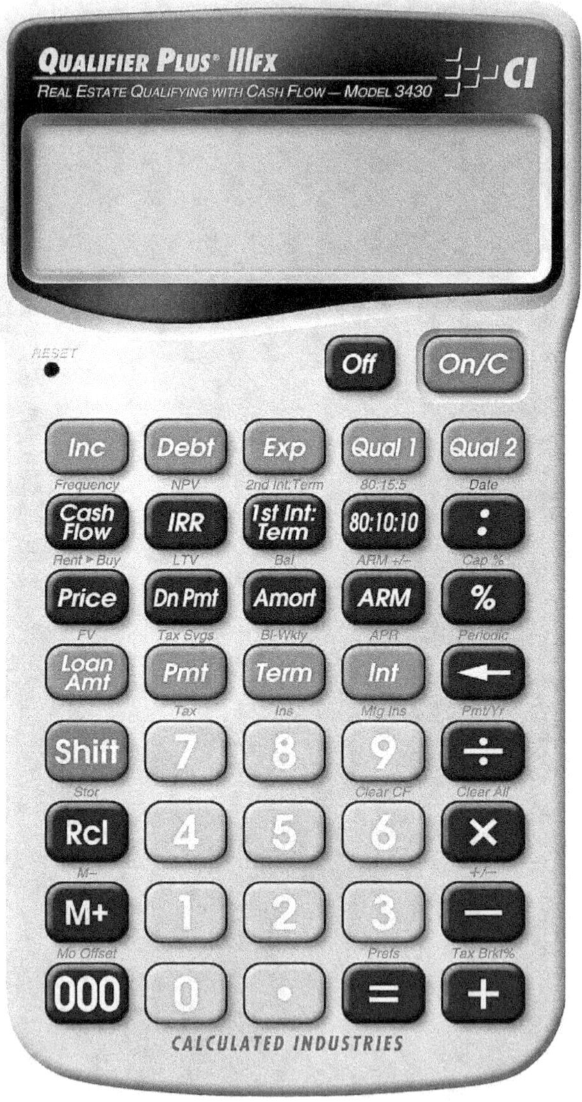

Pyramid of a Complete LO

Loan Comparison Chart

	USDA	VA	FHA	CONVENTIONAL
Max Financing	100%	100%	96.5%	97%
Financing Closing Costs	Yes	No	No	No
One Time Fee (Financed)	Guarantee Fee 1.0%	VA Funding Fee 0-3.6%	Financed MIP 1.75%	Varies
Monthly Fee	.35%	N/A	.85%	Varies
Bankruptcy (Waiting Period)	3 Years	2 Years	2 Years	4 Years
Foreclosure (Waiting Period)	3 Years	2 Years	3 Years	7 Years
Short Sale (Waiting Period)	3 Years	2 Years	3 Years	4 Years
Seller Concessions	6% of the sales price	No cap on closing costs, but 4% cap towards pre-paids and other items	6% of the sales price	• 3% with < 10% down • 6% with ≥ 10% down • 2% cap for investment properties